How to work with microbusinesses

Advice and
guidance
for providers
of training and
business support

Acknowledgements

The ADAPT FESME VCU project partners are indebted to many people who gave their time to assist in creating constructive ways to forge closer community relationships between the FE sector and the smaller employer sector.

College representatives have assisted in various ways. They responded to the first national survey of college views on working with microbusinesses in autumn 1998. The project survey also sought views on Ufi and was followed by a national survey that sought views on the new Small Business Service. College representatives also attended events on related issues, including the project's three events during March and April 2000. Although acknowledgement of particular colleges' involvement risks unfair exclusion, special thanks are due to Barnet College, Farnborough College of Technology, Filton College, Gateshead College, MANCAT, Oldham College, Rotherham CAT, Somerset CAT and Stockport College of HE and FE. These colleges all informed and influenced the project work, as have representatives from many ADAPT projects, including the Marchmont project.

The ADAPT FESME VCU project is also indebted to representatives from microbusinesses who gave their time in interviews organised through colleges and in representation of membership organisations comprising microbusinesses across all sectors, and groups of smaller organisations providing specific services, from accountancy through residential care to outdoor recreation.

Lastly, the ADAPT FESME VCU project thanks the TUC, for its interest in encouraging real employment opportunities in a 'market economy'.

Introduction

The ADAPT FESME VCU project's aims and work

Aims

The ADAPT FESME VCU project encourages colleges, and other educational and training agencies delivering business support, to work effectively for microbusinesses and suggests that appropriate tools and targeted funding are required to achieve this. It proposes national policies to enable colleges to maintain their community-based focus, so that they can help microbusinesses to grow.

Funding and partners

The project was funded by the European Social Fund (ESF) from September 1998 to December 2000, to research the relationship between FE colleges in England and Wales and their local, small and medium-sized businesses (SMEs). Project partners included: Apple UK, BAE SYSTEMS, FEDA, ICL and the Open University. Associate partners included: Ufi Ltd, Open College of the North West, IRISI (NW Regional Assembly), the North West Development Agency, and the North West Aerospace Alliance (NWAA, a membership group of employers in the defence and aerospace sectors). Several colleges are involved in further work with the project.

Project work

The project undertook the first national survey of all FE colleges' activity with SMEs in England and Wales and has since produced a website, and guidance for colleges' work with microbusinesses and SMEs. A final event was held to debate how to take forward the project's work once it had ended.

There has been an emphasis on the demand side in all the work; for example, the project considered the views of:

- the smaller firms surveyed quarterly by the Small Business Research Trust (SBRT), an independent research body

- the Northern Council of Outdoor Education, Training and Recreation, and of commercial members of Tourist Boards
- accountants who are members of the Group Practitioners Board of the Institute of Chartered Accountants, who know the practical reasons why the smaller firms they serve are often unable to sustain the employment they provide
- the TUC, where concerns for employees in smaller firms were raised during the recent work on the Employment Relations Act
- local, regional and national associations of care homes.

The project's transnational work concentrated on the care sector because of the preponderance of small, private nursing homes. These are required by law to comply with regulations covering staff qualifications and are experiencing significant challenges brought about by changes in demography, legislation and working practices. They thus provided a useful example in microcosm of the pressures on SMEs subject to radical change in their sector.

Since 1998, the project has monitored the views of those listed above, elicited views of businesses through users of ICL's CyberSkills Centres and a group of businesses in South Wales, and consulted with colleges and other providers. There are clearly good reasons for the difficulties experienced by both SMEs and providers in establishing working links; for example, NWAA commented that the FE sector does not routinely make it easy for employers to find out what services it offers. Similarly, interviews with smaller firms undertaken by colleges engaged in EU-funded projects revealed that EU-funded work was made more difficult because of smaller firms' inability to provide private matched funding. Concerns about the lack of focused national policies on 'connectivity' issues were also recognised.

The project is now undertaking a national survey with the SBRT on smaller firms' views of training issues. This survey will determine how smaller businesses may be motivated to use publicly funded business support services, ranging from the current Small Business Service to the many learning initiatives such as Investors in People (IIP), Individual Learning Accounts, etc.

Emerging issues

- Colleges' unique role in the local community should be acknowledged and encouraged. With the right tools and targeted funding, Further education is ideally based to forge relationships with local, small firms; to help them evaluate different learning services; and to gather their views, to inform local, regional and national policies, standards and systems. Colleges already collaborate with local and regional bodies, including parts of their region's development agencies and Training and Enterprise Councils (TECs) and Business Links (to be replaced by the learning and skills councils) and the Small Business Service (SBS) respectively. They may also collaborate with regional parts of national organisations, including Ufi and NTOs.

- Publicly funded business support services and training providers should promote the business benefits of their services. They need to recognise that business owners and managers of microbusinesses undertake full 'corporate responsibility' for all aspects of the company, including personnel, financial, and regulatory issues. This is often overlooked in initiatives for change, including those on e-commerce, competitiveness and lifelong learning, and results in unrealistic proposals.

- National, regional and local acknowledgement should be made of microbusinesses' vulnerability in a 'market economy'. Appropriate policies could be adapted to nurture firms and help them continue their economic activity and protect local jobs. The policies need to help firms to address practical issues, such as securing work from larger organisations, using computerised facilities more effectively and gaining knowledge of 'productivity' issues, so that they can set fair conditions for equitable reward, without recourse to job losses.

- Employers' views need to be gathered effectively on business-related issues, including the commercial and administration problems of providing private matched funding for publicly funded project work. These views need to be properly disseminated to regional intelligence units (RIUs) within Regional Development Agencies (RDAs), the Small Business Service (SBS) and the National Training Organisation (NTO) National Council, the sector-specific NTOs, and those starting regeneration-related projects.

- The SBS and NTO National Council need to work together on issues relevant to most small firms including: reduction in the cost of workplace assessments and development of more appropriate national standards. Initiatives instigated by the Department of Trade and Industry (DTI) should be similarly co-ordinated with those from the Department for Education and Employment (DfEE).

- Antidiscriminatory policies are needed on computerisation issues such as connectivity and band-widths, so that workplace improvement and regeneration-related initiatives can make practical use of information and communications technology (ICT).

- 'Best value' in national publicly funded business support and workplace training should be better defined and judged by rigorous quality criteria that take account of the small firm context, in terms of benefit for those receiving the services. The success criteria should include real and sustainable 'productivity improvements', such as increased outputs or reduced use of valuable resource. Criteria must be fair and achievable by people working in large firms and SMEs but secure equal quality of provision.

- The SBS and RDAs, informed by RIUs, need to develop interventions that enable 'mixed markets' to work effectively. The training and business support market is an example of a 'mixed market'; it delivers state services, served by public, independent, voluntary and private sector providers. An analogous example of a mixed market is care provision to the elderly, where 'best value' should be measured in terms of equitable provision to an increasingly frail, elderly population.

- Consideration of incentives, such as tax breaks and loans for training, may be needed for smaller firms, so that they can include their 7m workers in learning and development. Initiatives such as individual learning accounts which promote the uptake of learning by individuals, are being supplemented in some TEC areas with contributions from the employer to secure workbased basic skills provision. Such combined efforts may be successful in enabling mutual benefits to employers and employees to be realised.

Context

Microbusinesses – firms of up to ten people – and small and medium-sized enterprises (SMEs) – firms of between ten and 250 people – are major providers of local jobs in the European Union. However, EU Member States acknowledge that microbusinesses 'have fewer resources to get to grips with government regulation and less opportunity to influence government thinking'.[1] Microbusinesses therefore need to be encouraged and supported to sustain and grow their provision of stable or 'core' jobs.

Local jobs in microbusinesses may be affected by changes in regulations or the closure of large local organisations. The problem may be compounded when large organisations stop placing small contracts with local smaller suppliers; a practice that has traditionally helped purchasers avoid single sources of supply, and also sustained local economies.

How to work with microbusinesses encourages partnerships between learning providers and microbusinesses by:

- providing a rationale to motivate the instigation of the partnership (see chapter 1)
- promoting awareness of the different types of partnership (see chapter 2)
- examining strategic policy-making and relevant good practice, for each of ten topic areas (see chapters 3–12).

By providing this advice, the publication should inform policy development and enable providers to develop good practice in working with microbusinesses.

Effective partnerships with providers should improve microbusinesses' competitiveness – one of the criteria of the ADAPT community initiative and of the European Union's European Social Fund (ESF). Unless providers of workplace learning and business support can assist firms to develop the 'know-how' to protect local jobs, many of the ESF's other key initiatives, 'to help the long-term unemployed, young job-seekers, people excluded from the labour market, and to promote equal opportunities' will not be possible on the scale now anticipated by the European Union.

Initiatives such as Ufi Ltd,[2] which aim to support learning and sustainable employability, are also central to greater social inclusion and a fairer society. Such initiatives, if comprehensive, can greatly encourage jobs in the microbusiness sector, by stimulating effective learning in workplaces. However, the initiatives would be enhanced if adapted to current conditions and matched with national policies to create a culture of job retention and 'sustainable employment', so that individuals can find jobs to use their talents and capitalise on their new skills or knowledge.

Characteristics specific to microbusinesses

Modest turnover – generally too small to set aside funds for investment in training and other support at levels that make such provision commercially feasible on an individual business basis.

Few specialist staff – they may therefore have difficulty understanding training and support terminology, so that evaluating such services takes great effort from both the microbusiness and the prospective provider. It may also mean that microbusinesses base their evaluation strictly on the perceived benefits to their direct business objectives, rather than, as in some larger concerns, on the indirect benefits to personnel and training functions.

Disproportionate cost of conformance to regulation – they are unlikely to employ legal and performance management practitioners (see above) and yet have to contend with many regulations designed for much larger organisations. These are likely to increase the investment required by microbusinesses wishing to grow and employ more staff.

Episodic involvement in formal training – generally this is related to immediate needs, although informal networking and information exchange may be a regular and frequent activity.

UK changes

Recent structural changes that affect partnership mechanisms between education and business include:

- From April 2001, the Learning and Skills Council (LSC) will be responsible for the management and delivery of post-16 education and training. Employers will contribute to the work of the new national Learning and Skills Council, to its local branches and to the proposed Small Business Service.

- Local delivery of support for SMEs[3] will be through 40–50 sub-regional 'franchises' on behalf of the Small Business Service, rather than through the current 80 Business Link Partnerships within the Training and Enterprise Councils (TECs).

- A new careers advice service for young people will be created, providing a comprehensive advice and support structure; this is complemented by the recent regulations for organisations employing staff aged 17–18.[4]

- The structure and core services of the Education and Business Partnerships are to be changed.

- Local lifelong learning partnerships[5] have been formed so that colleges, schools and local authorities can ensure that there are effective local arrangements for post-16 workplace development, lifelong learning and careers guidance. Their success should be measured in improved local economies.

How to work with microbusinesses

1 Mutually beneficial partnerships

The 1997 Competitiveness White Paper noted that partnership enables bodies and individuals to work together to achieve different but mutually desirable objectives, including that of sharing workplace goals.[6] Partnership can also indicate the willingness to work inclusively with everyone with something to contribute. This inclusive interpretation is key to the provision of effective support to microbusinesses, especially as financial returns may be small.

'Partnership' encompasses relationships for different purposes. These may be:

- commercial and employment
- regulatory
- community.

Partnership for commercial and employment purposes is perhaps the most straightforward. Mutual benefit needs to be involved, otherwise partners are unlikely to give their greatest efforts to joint objectives such as performance, growth and job protection.

Partnership for regulatory purposes is different in that the impetus for collaboration is external and may not be owned by participants. The 'mutual benefit' in this type of partnership can be measured by local businesses and enforcers working in harmony, to the good of local employment conditions and opportunities.

Partnership for community purposes may involve a partner from the education sector requesting a contribution from business to develop a product or service. The businesses may gain publicity or staff development. More often, benefits are intangible and long term. For instance, where a business provides a teacher placement, the community may benefit in the longer term, with future school leavers better briefed about the world of work and local employment opportunities. However, now that even large businesses have less time for such activities, it is understandable that very few smaller businesses can become involved. Many good projects, especially those based on private-sector matched funding, fail to secure funding and companies have become wary of releasing confidential costing details, especially now that information can be exchanged between government departments.

Colleges are very positive about fostering sustainable relationships with microbusinesses in communities with a decreasing proportion of larger employers.[7] They are working in partnership, to the benefit of the local economies,[8] delivering training and education to post-16 year olds, to prepare them for employment. As local, well-established organisations, colleges have good reasons to overcome any barriers and create good relations in order to:

- secure work placements for their students
- protect and develop good local jobs by delivering training and mentoring in local workplaces
- gather local employers' views and represent them to regional and national initiatives possibly to secure development projects, funds, etc.

The key issues in creating mutually beneficial relationships affect most firms and most of their providers, whether they are educational establishments, agencies or associations supporting business or commercial providers, so the 'good practices' outlined here are fully transferable over the whole sector providing support to microbusinesses.

ACTION POINTS
Mutually beneficial partnerships

List the college's existing partnerships with microbusinesses, including those maintained by college staff in subject areas, by the college's Business Development Unit and by those in the college who deliver publicly funded initiatives on, for example, ICT and basic skills.
  Categorise the partnerships by their different activities, such as:

- college delivery of short-course learning services by subject area
- college delivery of longer courses in the college for employees on block release, and for apprenticeships
- college delivery of New Deal placements and other government initiatives
- microbusinesses' provision of work-placements for college students, of college governors, of mentors for students' projects, and for other involvement in students' projects, perhaps through the Neighbourhood Engineer scheme
- forums for determining employers' views on provision.

Analyse the above list and note where there may be duplication or gaps. Review policies to instigate more effective ways of keeping in contact with local employers.

List the college's commercial activities and note where they may conflict with partnership activities. Review policies on commercial activities, for example catering or advisory services, to ensure that they are not in unfair competition with local small businesses.

Ensure that the cost of partnership activities – in terms of financial outlay and staff time – is documented. Raise these resource issues with the appropriate bodies to ensure they are aware of the college's contribution and the resources required to sustain partnerships.

2 Reasons to help microbusinesses

Microbusinesses provide valuable employment and make a significant contribution to the local and national economy. Colleges with a community mission may prioritise work with microbusinesses because of their importance to local employment and social cohesion. Colleges with a focus on skills development may not immediately see microbusinesses as a key target group, but should consider how they may add to the support of other providers, in terms of specialist resources or expertise. There is unlikely to be financial profit for the assisting organisation. Making the initial contact, determining precisely what assistance each individual firm needs, developing and staffing the services, all require investment.

A key good practice for those who sell services to microbusinesses, must be to ensure that they provide effective assistance. Beneficial partnerships with other local and regional providers and agencies may:

- reduce the costs of provision to microbusinesses by providing complementary services across the area or region, or by offering training to clusters of small numbers of learners from different companies
- improve the gathering and representation of microbusinesses' views, as individual agencies and authorities have traditionally focused on the views of larger employers, whose representatives are easier to contact.

Barriers

Ideally, partnerships need to be forged before services are launched as working relationships between the collaborators have to be developed, perhaps reviewing traditional roles and generating new ones.

Some microbusiness employers may worry about organisations that offer publicly funded assistance, because of unsatisfactory past experience or simply 'fatigue' from continual changes in state-driven support networks.

There is a popular misconception, mostly unearned, that microbusinesses exploit their staff. They are unlikely to have a culture of redundancy to increase short-term profit. Unlike the employer in a larger organisation, a microbusiness employer is the firm's executive manager, overseeing the whole direction of the business, involved in the day-to-day running of the firm, and often knowing everyone on the payroll.

Advantages

Microbusiness shareholders usually have the firm's long-term interests at heart. Their livelihoods are likely to depend upon its success so they may take relatively small dividends to re-invest profit, or surplus and are unlikely to be representatives of 'unseen' investment fund managers.

Another advantage of microbusinesses is that they can often make quick decisions about, for instance, adapting to market opportunities or purchasing training, because management and staff can communicate without the bureaucracy of inter-departmental meetings and without being spread over different buildings.

Difficulties in helping microbusinesses

A high, and increasing, proportion of the UK's firms are microbusinesses (see Appendix 1). These smaller organisations usually have much lower annual turnover and profit margins than a larger organisation and difficulty raising capital.[9]

The officially calculated average turnover of £200,000 or more, per annum, for the UK's smallest firms, suggests a misleadingly positive economic position. An annual turnover of £200,000 may be reached by microbusinesses, like tobacconist–newsagents which sell from stock but may make little profit. Microbusinesses selling services involving little stock may turn over much less.

There are overheads in running any firm. If overhead costs are divided by the number of people working in a firm, this apportionment of overheads compared with individual gross salary can be much higher in a small firm. Consequently, managers in microbusinesses can be motivated to rationalise their overhead costs, rather than their staff costs, to improve their chance of survival and their profit margins.

Many small firms survive on very low profit levels. Market pressures are likely to increase the proportion of firms turning over much less than £232,000 per annum and the failure rate is high. The UK and other European Member States have already lost too many established businesses and jobs. Helping microbusinesses to flourish could indirectly extend local employment and reduce social exclusion. Providing appropriate and accessible learning solutions to business problems may greatly assist the sustainability of microbusinesses.

ACTION POINTS
Reasons to help microbusinesses

→ Identify microbusinesses for whom the college provides goods or services. Subgroup voluntary sector and private firms by trading or business interest. Analysis of the list may re-focus the college's work on partnerships with particular groups of employers, perhaps in specific sectors.

→ Consider repeating this listing exercise for organisations that the college worked with five or ten years ago. This could indicate trends in local employment patterns and influence future priorities.

→ Ensure that regional authorities, like the Regional Development Agencies (RDAs) and Learning and Skills Councils (LSCs), value colleges' community involvement and assist in forging relationships between colleges and 'official' organisations, like local authorities, the Small Business Service and national training organisations.

3 Investing in microbusinesses

When investing time and resources in providing assistance to microbusinesses, it may be helpful to understand the basic principles of productivity measurement and performance management.

Productivity

In simple terms, productivity may be measured by the ratio of output over input. Production, a term often used mistakenly for productivity, is only one of the output elements, albeit an important one. Employee costs form part of the input. Investment resource is another input element. Productivity ratios and indices may be improved by increasing the output relative to the input, or conversely, worsened by increasing the input relative to the output.

Productivity can also be seen in the wider context of social inclusion. For instance, the resource invested in lifelong learning initiatives, such as ADAPT (an input), needs to achieve an increase in productivity through, for instance, the number of jobs it helps to create or protect (an output). Many earlier partnerships failed to deliver 'outputs' in terms of jobs, despite improving collaboration between public-sector delivery agents.

Investing in provision

The key issue in building provision of assistance for microbusinesses is that it takes a great deal of investment, in capital terms and in long-term relationships with local employers and communities. Colleges and support agencies may already have made an investment including:

- developing courses to enable learners to accumulate credit towards recognised qualifications
- nurturing collaborative and partnership arrangements, which increase the effectiveness of provision to local employers and employees

- improved internal on-line systems or enhanced marketing work, for instance, constructing websites with partners or developing electronic course directories
- opening Outreach centres to enable more convenient learning
- employing and developing staff with appropriate skills for microbusinesses, and for training trainers, advisers, mentors, tutors and assessors for microbusinesses, perhaps within specific industries
- integrating ICT into the supply of assistance to microbusinesses
- software materials and collaborative development of new materials.

Improving sustainable productivity

At an individual company level, any work-based training or assistance should aim to improve the real and sustainable productivity of the organisation by reducing the overall 'input' or by increasing the 'output'. Often this is not easy: the company may want assistance or training in one area, when the problem is somewhere else. For example, a company might request a training course in stock control for an employee when the problem of high stocks lies elsewhere. No reputable provider of assistance to microbusinesses can take lightly the responsibility of recommending the 'wrong' course; jobs can be at stake unless underlying business problems are addressed.

Lifelong learning initiatives that target learners in the workplace also need to ensure that 'improving productivity' starts to be recognised as a 'friendly' action.

Performance management

A focus on performance management would further improve provision of support to microbusinesses. This will involve assessment of their performance against subjective or objective criteria, for instance:

- an individual or a sector's effectiveness
- an overall organisation's or sector's success.

In a working environment, good performance management will:

- be crucial to remaining competitive
- result in real and sustainable productivity improvements and job protection, preferably without causing unemployment elsewhere

- result in congenial working conditions and equitable payment/reward
- ensure sustained and beneficial services, for instance, increased performance levels and the expansion of economic activity in the locale. It should not be measured solely in singular or subjective terms like 'better use of computerised resources' within the business or 'improved collaboration' between agencies.

For owner/managers of microbusinesses, good performance management also needs to:

- ensure a profit margin. If no profit margin is achieved, the firm risks trading illegally, while insolvent
- protect jobs. Making staff redundant is particularly dreadful in small firms where staff are personally known and the loss of skilled resource can undermine the whole concern.

Because small businesses are likely to be approached by different agencies for a range of initiatives, it may be difficult to assess the benefits arising from any one, specific intervention. Care therefore needs to be taken when selecting performance management criteria.

Implementing change

Implementing change requires investment, if not in money, in time, to understand what needs to be adapted to ensure that the organisation survives. It takes staff time in any size of organisation, but is likely to take disproportionate key management time in micro-businesses.

ACTION POINTS
Investing in the productivity of microbusinesses

For each partner (as listed in the action points at the end of Chapter 2 on page 16), estimate how much resource has been spent building and working in that partnership, and how much benefit has been gained – in financial terms, in student numbers, in students that have left college and gained local jobs, or in other appropriate terms.

Partnership flourishes when all partners feel that they benefit, so consider the benefits gained by your partner(s), using objective and realistic indicators. Privately owned firms indicate benefits received by paying for college services, requesting further services (i.e. repeat business) and recommending the college's services to other firms (i.e. making referrals).

4 Gathering the views of microbusinesses

Gathering the views of microbusinesses is crucial to ensuring that effective and relevant local services are available to them.

Information sources

There is a mass of labour market information gathered by national or regional government agencies, and private or voluntary sector bodies.[10] Intelligence can be gathered first hand through local employer liaison groups and in consultation with local firms and strategic partners, so that banks of local and regional information regarding skill gaps, employment trends, and industry needs are developed. Many UK organisations do their own market research on microbusinesses as:

- surveys often cover only larger local employers
- only a few surveys represent microbusinesses' interests. (See Appendix 3.)

There are few cogent sources of microbusinesses' views in the UK[11] but where they exist, their key findings remain current. For instance, on the array of initiatives and schemes aimed at small firms:

There is no lack of advice around. The Business Links concept is right, but don't spend money on infrastructure which may not be needed.[12]
Barriers to growth (1996)

Information methods

It can be time-consuming to develop a customised small firms questionnaire. It might well be more effective to use in-depth interviews with a representative group (see Appendix 4), than to telephone firms or mail survey questionnaires speculatively. The in-depth approach allows the interview to be recorded, and can be very fruitful.

Survey forms and diagnostic tools can also be used for in-depth questioning. Running a small business can grant great freedom, but it can also be lonely. Questioning by someone outside the business can help to combat isolation, and enable a business owner to review their business, or develop new thoughts or ideas. This questioning needs to be undertaken sensitively however, as business confidence is crucial.

ACTION POINT
Gathering the views of microbusinesses

Check how the college keeps up to date with local employers' views.

- Does it draw on findings of the Small Business Research Trust (SBRT) or other sources of practical, independent views, gathered directly from microbusiness?

- Does it draw on the information available from helplines for firms – these can indicate relevant trends and current areas of concern to firms, while retaining confidentiality of individual firms' details?

- Does it make best use of informal contacts with employers, such as small business clubs, networking activity, etc.

5 Optimising local provision for employers

Preparing for new legislation

When preparing for change, employers with microbusinesses, like any others, consult their accountants, bankers, insurance brokers or legal specialists. Some may also receive free advice from their 'business angel' or venture capitalists. They may use assistance from state-driven bodies, including:

- colleges and other educational establishments
- Business Links (which may be part of Chambers of Commerce)
- trade-related agencies, like Tourist Boards
- regulatory bodies at local and regional levels, especially those with an additional advisory role
- helplines, websites and other national information services.

Optimising the use of public funds requires effective central guidance, perhaps by Regional Development Agencies in conjunction with regional government offices. Because the income stream generated from providing assistance to an area's microbusinesses may not even cover the cost of organising delivery, consistent but possibly low-level funding for support is important to ensure that:

- provision can be planned and co-ordinated with all agencies for effective, complementary and sustained provision
- there is a delivery infrastructure over an area, sustainable on minimum contribution from microbusinesses.

Forward-planning

Forward-planning is a key element of local co-ordination of support for SMEs. Early 'awareness-raising' initiatives can ensure that practical assistance is available for individual firms, in terms that employers can understand. 'Early start' work, through seminars and articles in local newspapers and trade magazines, raises awareness of new regulatory requirements in the developers and organisers of local support. They then have time to arrange assistance for local employers in implementing the new requirements.

Co-ordinating approaches

A major barrier to achieving an effective interface between local employers and providers of education, support and training is the sheer number of initiatives requiring employer involvement.
    As an example of the array of separate initiatives, colleges target employers to:

- offer support and basic skills training, which can directly help their businesses
- request sponsorship of specific projects and donation of equipment for example, which may only help their businesses indirectly in the short term, in the promotional sense of being involved in the community
- request firms' time in the form of representatives to serve as governors and as mentors, for instance within Project Enterprise projects and engineering-related schemes
- provide work placements for staff and students – a key form of partnership between education and business.

Much work has gone into forging partnerships between education and business. Some larger firms have made substantial commitments on a recurring basis, for example providing work experience placements over a number of years. Microbusinesses, however, are not able to be as generous with their time and resources.
    All these partnership activities need to be co-ordinated, and multiple requests to particular employers reduced to avoid duplication or confusion. Those in the education sector also need to remember that asking firms for their free involvement, however helpful to the common good over the long term, can be incompatible with 'competitive' selling of the education sector's services to the business sector.

Researching other provision

There is a very encouraging breadth of projects and initiatives within local business communities, often involving colleges. Many colleges have built on their strengths and adapted their traditional cultures to provide successful new ways for people in microbusinesses to access learning; their work should be disseminated. By researching colleagues' work, colleges in the same area may be better placed to collaborate, reduce their initial investment costs and optimise their on-going costs. There is great potential for disseminating appropriate information about such work to a wide audience in colleges and in other interested organisations.[13]

Outputs from Ufi Ltd and the Small Business Service should also be researched as they:

- help identify and source essential materials and broker development and provision of such materials
- help develop effective solutions for workplace training and development in microbusinesses
- help colleges and local communities to benefit from a strengthened 'brokerage' service for course information, guidance, and progression in relation to assistance for smaller workplaces
- improve the awareness and credibility of the NVQ system and its associated standards.

As the provision of support for microbusinesses may reap little profit for the individual provider, it is essential to avoid duplication.

Making effective use of ICT infrastructures

Another way in which regions can co-ordinate their investment, is to ensure that separate investments in computers and facilities to access computer-based materials are used to the benefit of the whole region. For instance, some colleges have created excellent computerised facilities, which could be used not only by their core students but also by part-time students from local workplaces. Information sources collated by regions and nationally need to be made available to as wide a user base as possible.

Microbusinesses' views on computerised facilities may be gradually changing, but access to local ICT facilities could speed this change by raising awareness of possible business benefits. The relatively high cost of investment in ICT may present too high a risk for small firms if potential benefits cannot be evaluated. Providers may also offer microbusinesses the opportunity to use and assess hard and soft ware, reducing the risk of purchasing unsuitable or over-hyped equipment or facilities.

Collaborative work needs to start before the specification and purchasing stages of communal ICT facilities, and continue through their implementation and lifetime.

Promoting on-going job opportunities

Employers in many sectors, including engineering, manufacturing, retailing and tourism, can be best assisted by raising awareness of job opportunities particular to their sector. In the past, larger local companies maintained such awareness and indirectly provided a pool of skilled people for the microbusinesses.

For commercial reasons however, larger firms may now prefer to run their own campaigns and not support national or regional campaigns relating to the sector as a whole. This may well be best for them but does not help the sector and puts the onus of raising the profile of local job opportunities on the sector's microbusinesses.

Raising awareness of job opportunities may need to start in primary schools, for instance to stimulate interest in taking science-related courses in later school or college life. It may also require local firms in the sector to group together, to determine what skills and qualifications are required and what possible career paths they can offer. For instance, an awareness-raising exercise for job opportunities in tourism could well involve the local Tourist Board, the local authority's economic development agencies and the local Chamber of Commerce to work with local colleges and employers. Awareness of the benefits of working in a smaller, local business may also have to be raised, so that young people know that there is a feasible alternative to joining a large company outside their preferred residential area.

ACTION POINTS
Optimising local provision for employers

→ Check what steps the college has taken to co-ordinate its approaches to local firms.

→ Ensure that staff have been briefed on how to recognise the value of specialised training to improve productivity and competitiveness.

→ Check that services to a local, smaller workplace have really benefited it. Check that staff have an open mind, asking what assistance would help workplaces, in terms of improving the employer's chances of maintaining or increasing staffing levels?

ACTION POINTS continued
Optimising local provision for employers

→ If a 'demand' arises that the college does not 'supply' or is not funded to supply, ensure that the college has a procedure to find a local supply where possible (for instance, through the Small Business Service). If no local supply is available, check what procedure there is to inform regional and national authorities of the unsatisfied demand.

→ Check how the college keeps up to date with statutory requirements on issues that are common to many local workplaces (e.g. health and safety, employment, data protection, human rights, disability-related issues and so on) so that it can develop effective services in these areas.

6 Developing learning solutions to improve business

Learning solutions for the workplace often need to be developed with the dual aims of meeting the learner's objectives and those of his or her employer. The term 'learning solutions' is used here to differentiate between an off-the-peg course and a learning activity which will enable a company to solve a business problem, and so become more effective. Providers should try to fulfil these different expectations.

Solutions for the workplace need to address business problems. In some cases this may mean an extremely focused activity. For microbusinesses, learning solutions need to be geared towards people who are not necessarily expert in current training assessment processes or the language of training. Where learning solutions are to be delivered with computerised facilities, developers need to be aware that some microbusinesses have little knowledge of computers, and sometimes a great wariness of them. Some of the most successful 'learning solutions' for microbusinesses have developed from initial provision of a service in the form of a meeting place away from working premises that allows owners to become familiar with computer kit and software packages.

At the least, training provision to smaller workplaces could supply:

- basic courses to achieve skills needed for greater efficiency
- courses that form parts of state-funded initiatives to introduce new legislation or to improve understanding of current legislation
- courses that address the first principles of performance management.

Smaller businesses may request assistance to resolve a symptom, rather than the underlying problem. Consequently, learning solution development, especially for microbusinesses, hinges on the services of experienced practitioners who can help to determine those underlying problems. (See also Chapter 11, page 44.) Diagnostic tools can stimulate the business owner to review what is happening, face the realities of the situation, and determine what 'learning solutions' could best help the business.

Learning solutions need to benefit firms in at least one of the following ways:

- assist them to determine areas that make them ineffective. For instance, management areas that could be delegated or administrative areas that could be sub-contracted, such as PAYE or VAT work. It could develop key procedures to organise delegating specific tasks to another person, perhaps a new, part-time employee
- reduce their trading costs perhaps through help with evaluating new computer facilities and implementing new processes. Firms may come to realise that they need a better understanding of basic accounting or performance management techniques before they can move on
- reduce their trading risks through assistance on regulatory issues.

Linking lifelong learning to better regulation

One of the most pressing concerns for microbusinesses is coming to terms with new legislation. The implementation of this can be improved by ensuring that there is effective assistance to help employers act as quickly as possible. (For further information, see Appendix 4, page 66.) The assistance could be deemed successful if the regulations were effective without diluting the performance of the business.

At a national level, regulation has the best chance of successful implementation if:

- details of new rules and regulations are available in good time, to enable employers to prepare
- official guidance is clear and unambiguous
- official guidance is backed up with awareness-raising initiatives and practical support.

Firms of all sizes need help with sound productivity improvement techniques, especially those that have not yet adapted to new technology.

Regional and local approaches

At regional and local levels, new legislation could best be put in place if:

- there were 'early awareness' seminars and press coverage so that those who assist employers may arrange for adequate local assistance in good time

- providers of support were geared up to focus on the new and current regulatory requirements that are common to many different sorts of employers, for instance, the Employment Relations Act 1999, the national minimum wage and working time regulations, health and safety, and company law
- support related to specific sectors
- there was local provision for firms which need to break through a regulatory threshold to grow, as without help, it could take a disproportionate amount of investment.

In summary, each new or changing set of laws stimulates employers to learn. Lifelong learning initiatives need to harness and build on such stimulation.

ACTION POINTS
Developing learning solutions to improve business

Colleges should:

→ develop a range of services, apart from training, connected with business development; for example, advice in cash flow, employment practice, recruitment, etc

→ collaborate with others in the region to deliver awareness-raising campaigns to promote services. Although they may feel that they are competitors, collaboration can be a most effective use of each individual college's resource.
   Some UK regions have already invested in such collaboration, to the benefit of colleges, employers, their workers and their region. The North West Aerospace Alliance, a membership organisation of employers in the aerospace and defence sectors, has commented that it can be difficult for employers in some regions to know what services the college sector offers

→ collaborate with others in the region, to focus on specific sectors of business. Such collaboration may result in each college specialising in different sectors, and may take considerable investment, but the benefits can be great. Colleges gain, as their resources can focus on particular sectors, and their staff do not need to be 'jacks of all trades'; local workplaces gain, as colleges' services can be well promoted and known by their good reputation; and regions gain, as better support may enable employers to sustain or increase their staffing levels.

7 Involving trade unions

Although the power of the trade unions has waned, some unions, especially those in the arts and broadcasting sectors, are active in resolving small business-related issues. Their motivation has been to protect their members' interests, as employers have changed their contractual arrangements from 'core' employment to term contracts or self-employment. A key aspect of the union work for these members has been the development of training services which are available to their members nationally, but accredited and supported by only a few, regional providers. This has set a precedence for other nationally available services to microbusinesses.

Other unions remain wary of assisting microbusinesses in their protection of jobs, lest it be misread as an attempt to increase their membership rolls.

If 'partnerships at work' are to succeed in meeting common and mutually agreed objectives, specific training is needed in:

- the principles of a partnership arrangements
- the specifics of joint working exercises, using appropriate techniques to achieve real and sustainable performance improvements without recourse to job loss or job degradation.

ACTION POINTS
Involving trade unions

→ Check whether the college knows about the practical work of trade unions for workers in very small firms. For instance, the Musicians' Union looks after its members who are deemed to be 'small businesses', in that they are freelances.

→ Check whether the college works with any local unions, to assist smaller workplaces in understanding the statutory requirement for allowing workers to vote on workplace representation. Although this requirement currently applies to a threshold of firms with more than 20 staff, the threshold may be reduced in the next few years. Any involvement with trade unions that motivates them to do something practical for workers in microbusinesses, has to be encouraged.

8 Stimulating demand for learning

'Demand' for learning from microbusinesses may appear to providers to be low because microbusinesses satisfy their own needs; for instance, through ad-hoc training with the employer/owner as mentor; networking with other small firms; reading about new government requirements; and getting advice from their professional advisers or a Business Link. More training may be requested once microbusinesses know that practical and effective provision is locally available. They are most likely to 'demand' assistance because they have an immediate need, and know the organisation they approach through its good local reputation.

Meeting standards

Microbusinesses frequently find the post-16 education and training system bewildering. the lack of clarity in the language of the standards within NVQs and the difficulty of obtaining copies of these to peruse in detail presents an initial barrier.

Mystery also surrounds the ways in which standards are applied and assessed.[14] For instance, NVQs are hard to implement in many firms, particularly smaller ones without training specialists.

Systematic types of standards, like ISO 9000 and the UK's Investor in People (IIP), require organisations to formalise and document work instructions and organisational details. Firms with four or five staff manage well with lower levels of formality and compliance with these standards can leave microbusinesses with inappropriately bureaucratic systems.

National training organisations (NTOs) have now been established by the government, with the official aim of covering more than 95% of the workforce. NTOs act as a focal point for training matters in their particular sector of industry, commerce or public service; their role is to ensure that the skill needs of their sector are being met, and that existing occupational standards are being set and new ones established.

NTOs are in dialogue with employers to ensure that the needs of business are fully taken into account in developing training-related policies. Including microbusinesses in this dialogue is important to ensure that occupational standards reflect the needs of small firms.

Training budgets

Microbusinesses may not have a formal training budget but they do spend time 'training', in the sense of researching and learning. Whether costed or not, a smaller firm's 'training budget' can include:

- researching and learning about everyday things within the firm, and its current and prospective customer base
- the time, telephone charges and purchase of guidance documents required to determine the practicalities of fulfilling current and forthcoming rules and regulations
- coaching and mentoring colleagues on an everyday basis
- researching possible new purchases, evaluating them and passing on knowledge
- locating providers of effective assistance, to maximise use of resources.

Providers need to take account of this underpinning investment and consider how it can be exploited in formal training provision.

Marketing lifelong learning

Initiatives encouraging lifelong learning need to define their target audience clearly. For instance, marketing lifelong learning to an individual could aim to motivate that person to start learning again, perhaps through stimulating an interest in a non-vocational pursuit. In this case, only the individual needs to be motivated. Marketing lifelong learning to people in the workplace may need to stimulate the employee on a topic which is vocational and is seen by the employer as one in which improvement would benefit the workplace performance. Different sizes of firm also need to be approached in different ways.

Lifelong learning and continuous up-skilling are at the heart of smaller enterprises, which need to adapt to new laws and changing marketplaces, and which work with a small margin of profit and a consequent need for a small margin of error. Unless microbusinesses invest in learning about the new legislation and how to implement it, trade and jobs are quickly lost or downgraded.

People in microbusinesses have found that new employment legislation has been brought in without practical initiatives to support their implementation, and this has left them needing to learn quickly, and largely at their own expense. Microbusinesses find it increasingly difficult to get small value loans to 'tide them over'; the risk of 'better times' arriving later rather than sooner may be rising.

Although larger organisations also have to learn to implement new employment laws, ensure conformance to company laws and undertake aspects of the employer's responsibilities, they usually do this with the backup of in-house expertise and with a budget for external specialists.

Marketing lifelong learning to those in the smaller workplace needs to focus on the benefits of learning in terms of survival, investment protection and risk aversion.

Training incentives

Some colleges have been able to overcome the barriers to designing, marketing and sustaining effective provision of learning services to microbusinesses and to stimulate effective relationships with them.[15] As these relationships are key to gathering the feedback that is essential to removing such barriers, there needs to be a mechanism by which microbusinesses' interest can be generated.

There may be a fundamental problem associated with the 'intervention culture', in that companies may take state-subsidised training rather than using their profits to invest in training. There is also some evidence that if services are of value, organisations will pay for them. This is demonstrated by the Business Links, where organisations pay for services, partly at subsidised prices.

Over the years, many partnership activities have been instigated between education and business. These will only be able to survive and thrive if greater care is taken to 'train' the business partners in the work involved in each activity. Willing businesses require briefings to ensure that the learner, the learner's educational establishment and the business have mutually agreed objectives. The work to achieve these joint objectives could be counted as 'training for business'. As trading conditions become harsher, the opportunity for business to enter into such activities reduces. As many areas now lack larger local employers, and depend upon their communities of smaller employers, something fundamental needs to be done to ensure that partnership activities continue.

The same is true of New Deal placements, where effective briefings are required for employers in microbusinesses – again a form of training in the broader sense. Providers could thus play an extremely useful role.

Another way of reducing the price of training is to introduce tax incentives. The principle of tax incentives for training may assist those in the education sector wishing to build relationships with local employers. The tax incentive principle could also be extended to cover time spent by firms in consultation with national and regional bodies.

Improvement in training may also result if, for instance, colleges, national training organisations and the Small Business Service consulted microbusinesses. It would increase the penetration of training and lifelong learning by:

- stimulating interest and demand through involvement in the consultation
- ensuring that there are training standards to help firms sustain jobs and to increase the effectiveness and well-being of those they employ.

If the key to lifelong learning initiatives is encouraging a training culture, rather than the precise number and types of qualifications gained, it would be useful if a nationally accepted, wider definition of training could be developed for tax incentive purposes, for instance to encompass the following:

- ISO 9000 and IIP – which require lifelong learning principles to be espoused by companies
- training leading to a recognised vocational qualification other than NVQs
- training leading to a units of a recognised NVQ or vocational qualification
- training using the Ufi's branded 'training packages'
- assessment of accredited prior learning (APL) leading to a qualification
- partnership activity between education and business, including firms' provision of teacher placements and work experience placements for students and school pupils
- in-house joint working projects aimed at improving productivity, performance and rational competitiveness, consistent with job retention and equitable payment/reward – as these will address appropriate training issues

- partnership activity involving consultation with representatives from NTOs and education and training bodies to gather employers' and employees' views
- partnership activity between the Small Business Service and microbusinesses which informs the development of policy at local or national level.

ACTION POINTS
Stimulating demand for learning

→ Review how recent training subsidies for SMEs have been used by the college in practice. Were they spent delivering a lot of courses to a few middle-sized organisations rather than to a more inclusive selection of workplaces, including smaller ones? Consider how this practice could change if the types of activities listed in this chapter were undertaken.

→ Consider ways of pricing provision for small firms which takes account of available subsidies, but requires some contribution from the employer, or employee. Ensure that pricing policies are transparent and consistent.

9 Forging new partnerships with microbusinesses

Microbusinesses generally contact providers either to resolve an immediate problem or to prepare for an envisaged situation; they then look for somewhere with a good local reputation. However, a good local reputation can take a long time to build but be lost very quickly. For instance, microbusinesses often see themselves as 'hands-on' and 'doers'; and do not readily accept those whom they see as teachers. Some colleges address this by establishing outreach centres in high streets or hosting economic regeneration days when local authorities, colleges and schools all exhibit. These may also overcome initial resistance to entering premises last attended as students or what are considered 'grand' (and state-funded) offices. Many college staff are even more pro-active – engaging in networking through small business clubs and relationship building in the business community.

New contacts

New contacts are best made for reasons that benefit both the provider and the microbusiness. The provider could offer to assist firms which are 'clustered' through shared interest, for instance firms in retailing, care, tourism, farming or engineering and manufacturing sectors. The provider could also assist in general issues that relate to many firms, for instance new employment or health and safety regulations. Selling training directly is unlikely to be effective; it can only really be marketed within a service which will bring tangible benefit to the learner, to the employer and to the college.

Promoting services

Providers may promote their services in many ways, ideally in conjunction with complementary services offered by other organisations in their region. They can use:

- broadcast campaigns
- press campaigns
- direct promotions
- introductory events, including short 'taster' sessions.

Introductory events enable firms to meet providers' representatives and see facilities in relaxed surroundings. Some providers maintain catalogues of what they offer on websites. This is effective but needs to be supplemented with paper-based information so as not to exclude the significant percentage of microbusinesses without access to the Internet.

In some areas, providers have a local initial point of contact dedicated to workplace assistance, which effectively co-ordinates assistance provided by colleges, Business Links, local authorities and other local partners.

Handling enquiries

Once an initial enquiry has been made, providers may organise their responses in different ways. In some colleges, facilitators in commercial units or centres of excellence may be dedicated to providing general guidance and signposting to all callers. Other colleges may refer their callers to an appropriate vocational subject specialist. Whoever picks up the initial enquiry has the difficult job of matching what the caller perceives they need to assistance that will benefit the learner in the workplace and their employer, at a cost which is acceptable to the provider's organisation. It is unlikely that this can be achieved without face-to-face discussion.

If the response is not handled quickly and well, an initial contact can soon be lost, possibly along with the provider's good reputation in the view of the caller. The smaller firm needs to understand what is being offered and at what price; if the proposed training or support activity remains difficult to understand, initial enquiries may come to nothing.

ACTION POINTS
Forging new partnerships with microbusinesses

→ List each part of the college that may have been contacted by staff from microbusinesses i.e. subject areas, the Business Development Unit, outreach centres or parts of the college set to deliver Basic Skills, New Deal or other workplace-related initiatives. From each college contact, collect details of contacts made with workplaces with ten or fewer staff. How well has the college responded to these contacts? Were the microbusinesses asking for assistance because of a crisis, or because they were planning for future needs?

→ Could the college better channel its queries received from smaller, local firms?

→ Could the college better monitor its contacts with microbusinesses?

→ Has the college ensured that it handles queries arising from a crisis within the microbusiness in a different way to the queries raised about future needs? The first type of query may need an immediate reaction that the college is not set up to provide, whereas the college may be well equipped to satisfy the second type of query, as it can be delivered in a properly scheduled manner.

→ Address any perceptions of 'poor reputation'. This sometimes requires changes to internal policies and practices but other current causes of poor reputation are nationwide– like the frustration caused by the bureaucracy and cost of the work-based assessment required for NVQ.

→ Colleges will need to keep up with official policies, for instance the NTO National Council's work to involve microbusinesses in NVQ-related issues, and to inform official policy-makers at regional and national levels, including those in the Small Business Service, where problem areas require action.

10 Delivering effective services

'Account managing' microbusinesses

Most colleges have set up dedicated business training facilities or commercial units to co-ordinate delivery of training and development to firms. Even though more is being delivered by distance learning and through outreach centres, personal contact remains essential in securing and maintaining interest. Personal contact enables the college to monitor the organisation and content of its provision for microbusinesses so that assistance remains practical and beneficial to the learners and to their employers' business. Brief visits to employers' premises and induction sessions for each student from the workplace may effectively stop students from feeling isolated and ensure that they are suited to independent learning.

Maintaining contact

Responsibility for maintaining contact with microbusinesses may lie with college staff in subject areas or with someone in the business development unit. The disadvantage of the former is that if a smaller firm wants training in a different subject area, the technical members of staff need to have the skills and knowledge to hand over to another teaching department. Teaching staff may also lack the required degree of commercial skill to handle the microbusinesses' enquiries fully. On the other hand, if the college has a Business Development Unit to maintain contact with its local microbusinesses, the Unit needs staff who can not only co-ordinate sales negotiations between the college and the prospective customer, but also communicate effectively with teaching staff to determine what the college can offer.

Working with microbusinesses is time-consuming, and can be frustrating and financially unprofitable. Even when microbusinesses realise that they require assistance, it can be difficult for them to determine what is appropriate and what is available locally.

If training, rather than information and guidance, is required, micro-businesses often hit a substantial barrier in judging the value of the proposed training and qualifications. They typically need assistance to ensure that course objectives match the potential trainee's needs, as well as their organisational needs. Training providers have to develop a sound understanding of applying standards to workplace training and to practical curriculum development, working in harmony with the appropriate NTOs and awarding bodies.

Providing services to firms has to be based on common commercial necessity, otherwise the recipient of the services is unlikely to purchase more and the service provider may suffer financially. Each small contract can take as much time to organise and administer as a much larger one. A large contract, upon which both parties depend for on-going commercial success, may run over an extended period; there is sufficient contract value to warrant full-time management attention, and time for the two parties involved to communicate properly. Small contracts, like those placed by microbusinesses for training, have too little activity to sustain the partnership between supplier and provider. Partnerships with each microbusiness can be difficult to 'account manage'.

Acceptable costs and standards

The account manager's role is to ensure that the provision to microbusinesses is at a cost and standard acceptable to the provider. Willingness to provide small firms with 'what they want, where they want it, when they want it', has to be tempered by financial and other constraints. Maintaining an acceptable standard of provision of workplace assistance to microbusinesses is not easy, and feedback from learners may well raise issues that undermine the provider's good local reputation but are costly to remedy. An accumulation of losses on many small contracts can be as devastating as one large loss; it is essential that 'quality procedures' are applied as rigorously to delivery to microbusinesses as they would be to delivery of large contracts.

Problems may arise even when the provider and the microbusinesses have invested resource in evaluating and selecting the appropriate courses to match the learner's course objectives with the micro-businesses' requirements. They can be due to delivery at a distance; the provider may fail to deliver at an agreed time; or the smaller microbusiness might hit a temporary 'crisis', taking the learner away from a scheduled session. Another 'distance' problem can arise from learners losing motivation when they require course guidance and find it difficult to ask for help, feeling remote from the provider's base.

Using the right staff

The account manager ensures that adequately experienced staff are available to deliver the training and assistance. It is essential to avoid using staff with no experience of working in or with microbusinesses. To ensure that the college can maintain its standards, it may well be best to have a policy of employing dedicated staff, and using external suppliers only in prescribed circumstances. This policy may be key, as those delivering to microbusinesses, especially through distance learning, need to have the vision and expertise to do the work and the loyalty to feed back to the college when problems arise.

Although there are strong social reasons to assist local employers, the account manager's role is also to ensure that services which become financially or technically unfeasible are redesigned or withdrawn, and services with positive feedback are considered for development.

Outreach work: effective business coaching

Delivering services to microbusinesses encompasses many skills. Some are new – like supporting students in the workplace on an ad-hoc basis by telephone or e-mail. Others are more traditional. Supporting learning in microbusinesses may involve one or more people and can include any mix of the following expert areas and tasks.

- specialist help with training needs analysis and training plans, to demonstrate that the training will enable profit levels to be sustained and, ideally, improved. Training solutions need to be compatible with initiatives in areas such as productivity and performance management, and consistent with job retention or expansion

- mentoring the workbased learner is key to ensuring that training and assistance are properly related to the learner's work. Mentors ensure that learners have the required entry or foundation knowledge, and can highlight where blocks of rigorous, technical learning are required, perhaps by day or block release. They can feed back to colleges where work-based learning modules have become too academic and inappropriate. They ensure that learners are happy with the content of their course and motivated to learn.

This is separate from a 'buddy system' of mentoring which will come more into play as computerised distance learning grows more common so that learners do not become demotivated by technology or isolation. Mentoring within the workplace should be encouraged but may require some training from the college

- mentoring for the NVQ system's requirements.
- technical advice to support learning process, for instance to resolve a computer hardware problem. Microbusinesses without staff with the relevant technical knowledge may have to rely on colleges for technological support
- delivery of teaching and tutorial work
- assessment, examination and moderation of provision leading to NVQs and other qualifications.

A comprehensive term for the all-inclusive role described above could be the Business Coach.[16] The role needs to be all inclusive because no one, including the smaller firm's owner/manager, has in-depth knowledge of all the issues which may need to be addressed. The firm may call for assistance on any one of a wide series of issues, and the Business Coach has to be able to respond effectively. In a purely commercial environment the co-ordination part of the Coach role might need a clear 'referral' element to ensure that relevant expertise is called upon where necessary.

In addition to the tasks above,[17] the representatives who deliver services to microbusinesses need to be able to gauge where to make a referral. In a college providing services they might refer to:

- another member of college staff
- regulatory bodies and national helplines
- Business Links or Small Business Service or services from appropriate commercial providers
- national training organisations and awarding bodies for assistance, as appropriate to standards and to qualification-related issues.

By making such referrals, the provider draws on all the potential services and the local microbusinesses receive the most practical and appropriate assistance. Such referrals make good commercial sense; for providers they avoid the expense of developing one-off services and so unnecessary expense is saved and microbusinesses get better assistance.

ACTION POINTS
Delivering effective services

→ Has the college got clear procedures to ensure that it refers microbusinesses to other providers, if it cannot satisfy their needs? Are staff aware of sources of specialist support? Consider producing a directory of these.

Are there procedures to ensure that the college estimates the cost of tailoring a service to a firm's particular requirements and ensures that no tailoring is agreed to, if the cost to the college is too high? Does the college have the controls to avoid promising delivery without due attention to the cost of that promise and the quality of the result?

→ Who within the college takes the 'account manager' role? Is information gleaned during informal meetings or discussions between an account manager and an individual microbusiness or group of them, fed back to the appropriate person? The information may, of course, concern dissatisfaction, but at least then the college has a chance to address it. On the other hand, the information gleaned can lead to a need, or 'demand', that the college can consider satisfying.

11 What to offer and how to measure its effectiveness

Many microbusinesses may require small amounts of training as a continuing drip-feed process, and may have great difficulty in committing to a training plan because their needs change rapidly. Others may plan their training after a business decision, for instance a capital purchase of equipment or a specific sales contract stipulating specific qualifications.

A realistic starting point is to offer microbusinesses a few key services, at a good standard, to be sustained over the long term; it will take time to build relationships and a good local reputation. The services could fall into one or more of the following categories:

- training and assistance with conforming to current and new regulation, and guidance in the selection and evaluation of appropriate training and awarding bodies[18]

- training and assistance in response to needs that have been gathered from a group of local microbusinesses[19]

- guidance to match available training standards to practical requirements, perhaps with a focus on those that will best nurture the staff in smaller firms[20]

- working to forge alliances between groups of microbusinesses, perhaps in the form of a user-group or 'cluster', where they trade within a specifically regulated sector or have some other common bond or goal.[21]

A critical element for success is the focus on sectoral partnerships between providers and defined target groups of microbusinesses with similar ranges of needs. The needs of microbusinesses differ in different sectors, and much time and effort can be wasted in trying to provide what becomes effectively a bespoke service for each business. By focusing on sectoral partnerships, the college can play to its strengths and develop credibility as a provider.

ACTION POINTS
What to offer and how to measure its effectiveness

➤ What services and partnership activities does the college offer microbusinesses? If services beyond those promoted are requested, what procedure does the college enforce to ensure that tailored services are to an acceptable standard, with well-defined learning objectives?

➤ What procedures does the college have to ensure that services offered have set objectives: to satisfy the potential learner's motivation in taking the service, and to satisfy his or her employer's motivation in paying it or in releasing the employee for the time required?

➤ How will the the improvement of the workplace learner's employer's business be measured? In terms of reducing risks associated with trading perhaps, as the service will raise the ability of the workers to implement a particular set of statutory requirements? Or in terms of enabling the business to expand its activities in some way, as the ability of its workers is increased?

12 New products for microbusinesses

Commissioning new courses or revising current ones is a costly exercise, sometimes with additional work in making appropriate submissions to academic standards committees or external awarding bodies. Doing it for microbusinesses may be even more expensive, as the course objectives need to be determined both from the workplace learner's perspective and from that of the employer's business. Costs can rise again if the new course is toincorporate embedded ICT facilities so that materials can be accessed away from the college or at times suitable for independent learning or reference.

Revising courses to integrate ICT is not straightforward, as presentation and assessment may need to be changed – simply putting existing materials onto a website is not a solution. The first cost to consider is the investment required to familiarise staff with how computer-based resources can enhance their courses. If staff are not happy with the facilities, the chances of embedding ICT successfully are greatly reduced.

There is a growing selection of packaged courses but even they require significant involvement of teaching staff, as they need to be evaluated before purchase and then integrated into courses. Unless staff are involved in the evaluation, they may not feel equipped or motivated to do the integration. During the evaluation it is worth asking to interview one (or more) smaller firm that has already used the package. This is likely to involve a site visit, but is worthwhile to ensure that the package has actually helped coursework and enabled the smaller workplace to improve its business performance or sustain its job provision.

The key to purchasing packaged courses or commissioning new ones is clear specification. It should include:

- course objectives
- course contents, and how these relate to curriculum and to national standards
- the processes by which the course is to be delivered and supported
- the processes by which course assessment will be made
- the points during the course at which learners will be assessed.

Staff must be involved in the decision to design and develop a new course. If ICT facilities are to be embedded, staff must be familiar with the courseware design criteria. Wherever possible, computerised 'development tools' should be considered, so that academic members of staff can effectively generate their own materials, at their own pace, and when they have time. Such tools could be as simple as word processor and drawing packages, so that course materials are well presented. Tools can also include software packages to assist in the production of learning materials which are to be accessed on computer by the student.

Ideally, learners in microbusinesses and their employers need to be involved in some of the initial specification work, to ensure that course objectives and delivery processes are practical and easy to understand. The ways in which the course will relate to standards and curriculum requirements must be embedded in the design stage, so that learners know what credit they may accumulate towards appropriate qualifications.

Key questions

- Are new materials and courses to be developed or purchased n response to local demand for which the college has no supply, or due to a strategic decision to stimulate demand?

- If the development or purchase is in response to local demand, is the demand from an individual company? If so, will the cost of implementing the course be recouped by income from that one company, or is income likely to arise from other companies which note the first one's success?

- If the development or purchase is to stimulate demand, have the additional costs of marketing the new course and of supporting the services until an income stream is developed, been considered?

- Is the development to produce or purchase new courses to fill gaps in provision or solely to incorporate ICT facilities into existing, proven courses? Both can enable new learners to access courses, and the latter may also reduce some costs, for instance of purchasing paper-based library and learning resources.

- Is the newly developed or purchased course to apply to very small firms, with fewer than five staff, or to those with around 50 staff? This is a key question, as the ways in which materials will be presented will differ for the two sizes of 'smaller firm', even though size is not always the controlling factor. For instance, most microbusinesses will wish to improve productivity, payment reward and performance management.

However, the learning materials required to achieve these objectives can be very different. Small businesses with 50 or more staff and a formal, or semi-formal departmental structure, usually require a different set of learning materials from the smaller firm with fewer than five staff and no formal departmental structure, where the owners and shareholders remain involved in the operational work.

- Although the materials are to be developed to assist microbusinesses, can the same materials be used to enhance the preparation of students for working life, either in the longer term after college or more immediately for students about to start their workplace assignment within sandwich courses? Being able to use materials for more students may enable a cost saving, making the initial investment more feasible.

- Has the evaluation of the work involved in developing new courses been undertaken on a fair and sound basis? If 'off-the-shelf' packaged solutions have been rejected in favour of 'bespoke solutions', has this been done on an objective basis?

ACTION POINTS
New products for microbusinesses

How does the college decide what new services to offer microbusinesses? If the new services are due to a stated need by local firms, how does the college generate the resource to develop and supply them? If the new services arise from the college deciding to 'commercialise' some specific knowledge in particular subject areas, how does it promote these 'active', rather than 'reactive' services? How does the college check that other colleges in the area do not already specialise in this particular knowledge? If no other local colleges provide the new service, does the college target firms in a particular sector, build up good reputation in that sector, and then consider wider promotion of the service to other sectors?

What is the college policy on developing new services that incorporate ICT? Does it have IT specialists who work with subject area and teaching staff to ensure that ICT facilities are used well and have educational value when integrated into a recognised course?

Are other, specific staff assigned to evaluate new services, from the perspective of ensuring that learners using the new services may gain recognised progression or full awards (this can also be fundamental for colleges funding purposes)? Does the college ask representatives from microbusinesses to test the new services that incorporate ICT, so that their views can be gathered? Is the relationship of the new provision to direct benefit to business clear, to ensure that employers are likely to release their staff willingly?

13 Action points: summary

CHAPTER 1
Mutually beneficial partnerships

■ List the college's existing partnerships with microbusinesses, including those maintained by college staff in subject areas, by the college's Business Development Unit and by those in the college who deliver publicly funded initiatives on, for example, ICT and basic skills.
    Categorise the partnerships by their different activities, such as:

– college delivery of short-course learning services by subject area

– college delivery of longer courses in the college for employees on block release, and for apprenticeships

– college delivery of New Deal placements and other government initiatives

– microbusinesses' provision of work-placements for college students, of college governors, of mentors for students' projects, and for other involvement in students' projects, perhaps through the Neighbourhood Engineer scheme

– forums for determining employers' views on provision.

■ Analyse the above list and note where there may be duplication or gaps. Review policies to instigate more effective ways of keeping in contact with local employers.

■ List the college's commercial activities and note where they may conflict with partnership activities. Review policies on commercial activities, for example catering or advisory services, to ensure that they are not in unfair competition with local small businesses.

■ Ensure that the cost of partnership activities – in terms of financial outlay and staff time – is documented. Raise these resource issues with the appropriate bodies to ensure they are aware of the college's contribution and the resources required to sustain partnerships.

CHAPTER 2
Reasons to help microbusinesses

- Identify microbusinesses for whom the college provides goods or services. Subgroup voluntary sector and private firms by trading or business interest. Analysis of the list may re-focus the college's work on partnerships with particular groups of employers, perhaps in specific sectors.

- Consider repeating this listing exercise for organisations that the college worked with five or ten years ago. This could indicate trends in local employment patterns and influence future priorities.

- Ensure that regional authorities, like the Regional Development Agencies (RDAs) and Learning and Skills Councils (LSCs), value colleges' community involvement and assist in forging relationships between colleges and 'official' organisations, like local authorities, the Small Business Service and national training organisations.

CHAPTER 3
Investing in microbusinesses

- For each partner (as listed in the action points at the end of Chapter 2), estimate how much resource has been spent building and working in that partnership, and how much benefit has been gained – in financial terms, in student numbers, in students that have left college and gained local jobs, or in other appropriate terms.

- Partnership flourishes when all partners feel that they benefit, so consider the benefits gained by your partner(s), using objective and realistic indicators. Privately owned firms indicate benefits received by paying for college services, requesting further services (i.e. 'repeat business') and recommending the college's services to other firms (i.e. making 'referrals').

CHAPTER 4
Gathering the views of microbusinesses

- Check how the college keeps up to date with local employers' views.
- Does it draw on findings of the Small Business Research Trust (SBRT) or other sources of practical, independent views, gathered directly from microbusiness?
- Does it draw on the information available from helplines for firms – these can indicate relevant trends and current areas of concern to firms, while retaining confidentiality of individual firms' details?

CHAPTER 5
Optimising local provision for employers

■ Check what steps the college has taken to co-ordinate its approaches to local firms.

■ Ensure that staff have been briefed on how to recognise the value of specialised training to improve productivity and competitiveness.

■ Check that services to a local, smaller workplace have really benefited it. Check that staff have an open mind, asking what assistance would help workplaces, in terms of improving the employer's chances of maintaining or increasing staffing levels?

■ If a 'demand' arises that the college does not 'supply' or is not funded to supply, ensure that the college has a procedure to find a local supply where possible (for instance, through the Small Business Service). If no local supply is available, check what procedure there is to inform regional and national authorities of the unsatisfied demand.

■ Check how the college keeps up to date with statutory requirements on issues that are common to many local workplaces (e.g. health and safety, employment, data protection, human rights, disability-related issues and so on) so that it can develop effective services in these areas.

CHAPTER 6
Developing learning solutions to improve business

Colleges should:

■ develop a range of services, apart from training, connected with business development; for example, advice in cash flow, employment practice, recruitment, etc

■ collaborate with others in the region to deliver awareness-raising campaigns to promote services. Although they may feel that they are competitors, collaboration can be a most effective use of each individual college's resource.

Some UK regions have already invested in such collaboration, to the benefit of colleges, employers, their workers and their region. The North West Aerospace Alliance, a membership organisation of employers in the aerospace and defence sectors, has commented that it can be difficult for employers in some regions to know what services the college sector offers

■ collaborate with others in the region, to focus on specific sectors of business. Such collaboration may result in each college specialising in different sectors, and may take considerable investment, but the benefits can be great. Colleges gain, as their resources can focus on particular sectors, and their staff do not need to be 'jacks of all trades';

local workplaces gain, as colleges' services can be well promoted and known by their good reputation; and regions gain, as better support may enable employers to sustain or increase their staffing levels.

CHAPTER 7
Involving trade unions

- Check whether the college knows about the practical work of trade unions for workers in very small firms? For instance, the Musicians' Union looks after its members who are deemed to be 'small businesses', in that they are freelances.

- Check whether the college works with any local unions, to assist smaller workplaces in understanding the statutory requirement for allowing workers to vote on workplace representation? Although this requirement currently applies to a threshold of firms with more than 20 staff, the threshold may be reduced in the next few years. Any involvement with trade unions that encourages them to do something practical for workers in microbusinesses, has to be encouraged.

CHAPTER 8
Stimulating demand for learning

- Review how recent training subsidies for SMEs have been used by the college in practice. Were they spent delivering a lot of courses to a few middle-sized organisations rather than to a more inclusive selection of workplaces, including smaller ones? Consider how this practice could change if the types of activities listed in this chapter were undertaken.

- Consider ways of pricing provision for small firms which takes account of available subsidies, but requires some contribution from the employer, or employee. Ensure that pricing policies are transparent and consistent.

CHAPTER 9
Forging new partnerships with microbusinesses

- List each part of the college that may have been contacted by staff from microbusinesses i.e. subject areas, the Business Development Unit, outreach centres or parts of the college set to deliver Basic Skills, New Deal or other workplace-related initiatives.
  From each college contact, collect details of contacts made with workplaces with ten or fewer staff. How well has the college responded to these contacts? Were the microbusinesses asking for assistance because of a crisis, or because they were planning for future needs?

- Could the college better channel its queries received from smaller, local firms?

- Could the college better monitor its contacts with microbusinesses?

- Has the college ensured that it handles queries arising from a crisis within the microbusiness in a different way to the queries raised about future needs? The first type of query may need an immediate reaction that the college is not set up to provide, whereas the college may be well equipped to satisfy the second type of query, as it can be delivered in a properly scheduled manner.

- Address any perceptions of 'poor reputation'. This sometimes requires changes to internal policies and practices but other current causes of poor reputation are nationwide– like the frustration caused by the bureaucracy and cost of the work-based assessment required for NVQ.

- Colleges will need to keep up with official policies, for instance the NTO National Council's work to involve microbusinesses in NVQ-related issues, and to inform official policy-makers at regional and national levels, including those in the Small Business Service, where problem areas require action.

CHAPTER 10
Delivering effective services to microbusinesses

- Has the college got clear procedures to ensure that it refers microbusinesses to other providers, if it cannot satisfy their needs? Are staff aware of sources of specialist support? Consider producing a directory of these.
  Are there procedures to ensure that the college estimates the cost of tailoring a service to a firm's particular requirements and ensures that no tailoring is agreed to, if the cost to the college is too high? Does the college have the controls to avoid promising delivery without due attention to the cost of that promise and the quality of the result?

- Who within the college takes the 'account manager' role? Is information gleaned during informal meetings or discussions between an account manager and an individual microbusiness or group of them, fed back to the appropriate person? The information may, of course, concern dissatisfaction, but at least then the college has a chance to address it. On the other hand, the information gleaned can lead to a need, or 'demand', that the college can consider satisfying.

CHAPTER 11
What to offer and how to measure its effectiveness

- What services and partnership activities does the college offer microbusinesses? If services beyond those promoted are requested, what procedure does the college enforce to ensure that tailored services are to an acceptable standard, with well-defined learning objectives?

- What procedures does the college have to ensure that services offered have set objectives: to satisfy the potential learner's motivation in taking the service, and to satisfy his or her employer's motivation in paying it or in releasing the employee for the time required?

- How will the the improvement of the workplace learner's employer's business be measured? In terms of reducing risks associated with trading perhaps, as the service will raise the ability of the workers to implement a particular set of statutory requirements? Or in terms of enabling the business to expand its activities in some way, as the ability of its workers is increased?

CHAPTER 12
New products for microbusinesses

- How does the college decide what new services to offer microbusinesses? If the new services are due to a stated need by local firms, how does the college generate the resource to develop and supply them? If the new services arise from the college deciding to 'commercialise' some specific knowledge in particular subject areas, how does it promote these 'active', rather than 'reactive' services? How does the college do its market research to ensure that other colleges in the area do not already specialise in this particular knowledge? If no other local colleges provide the new service, does the college target firms in a particular sector, build up good reputation in that sector, and then consider wider promotion of the service to other sectors?

- What is the college policy on developing new services that incorporate ICT? Does it have IT specialists who work with subject area and teaching staff to ensure that ICT facilities are used well and have educational value when integrated into a recognised course?

  Are other, specific staff assigned to evaluate new services, from the perspective of ensuring that learners using the new services may gain recognised progression or full awards (this can also be fundamental for colleges funding purposes)? Does the college ask representatives from microbusinesses to test the new services that incorporate ICT, so that their views can be gathered? Is the relationship of the new provision to direct benefit to business clear, to ensure that employers are likely to release their staff willingly?

Appendix 1

Official statistics for the UK's firms

Table 1 indicates the high proportion of UK's firms that are microbusinesses, with fewer than ten staff.[22] Organisations with no employees include self-employed sole traders.

Table 1 The profile of the UK's employment, by size of business

Size (no. of employees)	Number of businesses	Employment (000s)	% Businesses	% Employment
None	2,339,645	2,749	64.0	12.7
1–4	922,585	2,356	25.2	10.9
5–9	204,290	1,483	5.6	6.9
10–19	111,800	1,568	3.1	7.3
20–49	48,300	1,496	1.3	6.9
50–99	14,945	1,043	0.4	4.8
100–199	8,145	1,127	0.2	5.2
200–249	1,520	338	–	1.6
250–499	3,215	1,123	0.1	5.2
500+	3,445	8,311	0.1	38.5
All	3,657,885	21,595	100.0	100.0

– negligible, assumed to be significantly under 0.1%.

There has been a recent increase in the number of microbusinesses and in the employment they provide, as indicated in Table 2 overleaf.

Table 2 How much the UK's firms turn over, and the changing business profile

Size (no. of employees)	Turnover (£m ex VAT)	Turnover/ Enterprise (£'000s)	Businesses % change Jan 97–Jan 98	Employment % change Jan 97–Jan 98
None	88,634	38	−7.3	−4.1
1–4	214,258	232	14.9	11.9
5–9	123,017	602	6.5	6.2
10–11	54,360	1,381	4.1	3.8
20–49	152,716	3,162	−3.4	−2.8
50–99	110,925	7,422	−3.0	−2.6
100–199	116,995	14,36	0.1	0.5
200–249	37,781	24,856	−3.8	−4.0
250-499	154,639	48,099	–	0.4
500+	773,663	224,576	1.0	4.0
All	1,926,987	527	−1.3	2.5

Chapter 2 discusses how turnover alone gives a misleadingly positive indication of the economic position.

Appendix 2
The UPBEAT project, Barnet College

The ADAPT UPBEAT project outlined in this appendix indicates the depth of work needed to gather small firms' views and organise effective support for their businesses. The project started in autumn 1998, and has succeeded in establishing effective, customised training and other support to local microbusinesses in North London, in the area of Barnet College.

The UPBEAT project focused on local microbusinesses in town centres, which are facing decline because of increasing competition from out-of-town retail and leisure developments. A high percentage of the in-town firms are owner-managed microbusinesses, employing fewer than five people. They include retailers, hairdressers, dry cleaners, equipment hire, opticians, shoe repairers, picture framers, motor-related firms, those in leisure, hotels and catering, letting agencies and financial services.

Barnet College embarked on the project with the primary aim of involving the college in its local communities; generation of income was not a key motive. The original plan was to deliver NVQs to small and medium-sized enterprises and to develop eight town locations.

First-hand data was collected from microbusinesses in the initial research phase, including:

- nature of business and current staffing levels, and whether they would be interested in free advice/training using IT to develop aspects of their businesses
- the most convenient times to receive advice/training, the preferred location and duration of such sessions
- whether the firms currently use computerised technology in their businesses, and if not, why not.

Further in-depth survey work gathered the firms' views on broader issues, including:

- take-up of locally delivered, state-instigated business support
- involvement with local larger firms, and in local networks and business associations
- how the project could play an effective role in local economic regeneration.

The project learnt hard lessons, including the following:

- microbusinesses largely reject NVQs. The 'European Computer Driving Licence' (ECDL) award, which has the British Computer Society's support, is more appropriate for computer and IT-related courses
- large committees of local partners are very time-consuming, as is the reporting process required by the ADAPT project funders
- public matched funding may not materialise in the time needed. Current private matched funding processes are also problematic, as the salary information required by funding authorities is commercially sensitive. Current private matched funding processes do not work for most very small firms.

The project succeeded in overcoming these problems. Its success was helped by senior officers of Barnet College recognising, before the start of the project, the need for the college to:

- make the long-term commitment to go out into the community and listen to those in its community
- take the long-term view to set up a business development unit with a remit for relationships with local firms, and then ensure that staff with commercial experience were employed to work in the unit, on the college's behalf.

The project continues to sell courses and deliver support to local firms through three centres, with a fourth one due to open. UPBEAT has built a core of microbusinesses interested in the support provided by the centres. The work of the project can thus be sustained by:

- continuing to sell some courses direct to microbusinesses
- developing a Business Club for microbusinesses, offering IT services to members
- tapping into appropriate publicly funded initiatives (which may be essential for further capital investment purposes). The major conclusions of the UPBEAT project have been incorporated in the main text of this handbook.

Details of the UPBEAT project survey work

The project needed to invest heavily in the design and subsequent development of its survey questionnaires. A questionnaire was designed for the initial postal survey, and then developed for the telephone, group and face-to-face interviews, to allow scope for additional information. Each questionnaire solicited the same core information, so that findings could be analysed systematically and comparisons made.

The postal survey, which raised awareness of the UPBEAT project, was followed by a great effort to encourage response. The subsequent telephone survey selected firms at random in the area, but excluded those that had responded to the postal survey. In a constructive analysis of its own work, the UPBEAT project realised that the following face-to-face interviews elicited little additional information but might have added more had they, for instance, focused on discussion of a specific computer package or some other practical point.

The project succeeded in gaining information from about 10% of the firms in the original postal surveys.

Of the 205 survey responses from one area surveyed:

- 135 firms (66%) had fewer than five staff
- 52 firms (26%) had between six and fifteen staff
- 8 firms (4%) had between sixteen and twenty staff
- 8 firms (4%) had more than twenty staff.

The firms that employed fewer than five staff represented 66% of those surveyed but 83% of the group that did not use technology for business purposes and 70% of the group that anticipated barriers to taking part in the UPBEAT programme.

General questions that were added to later versions of the survey questionnaire included those determining:

- how long businesses had been trading
- how many business owners had run businesses before the current owner (and whether their earlier businesses remained in their control, or had been closed down, sold, stolen, bought out or merged within another firm)
- whether firms considered that their businesses were less or more profitable compared with two years ago
- whether firms felt that their trading levels would improve, deteriorate or remain the same in the next couple of years.

As far as training and support were concerned, firms stated their preference for such services:

- on Tuesdays, Wednesdays and Thursdays, rather than Mondays, Fridays or at the weekend,
- in short sessions of up to two hours For half a day, ideally from 10am to noon, from 2pm to 4pm, or 6pm to 8pm.

The lack of staff time and cover were the major reasons given for non-participation.

Of the 310 responses when firms were asked to state their business use of computerised functions:

- 108 firms (35%) used word processing
- 60 firms (19%) had computerised invoicing
- 40 firms (13%) had some computerised stock control
- 70 firms (23%) had computerised accounting

- 32 firms (10%) used computers for purposes other than those listed above.
- 15 firms made no response, and a significant number indicated that they felt their businesses had no need for computerised technology.

The barriers to becoming computerised were given by 77 firms, as follows.

- 21 firms (27%), the cost of purchasing
- 9 firms (12%), the cost of training
- 25 firms (32%), lack of advice and information to evaluate computerised solutions
- 22 firms (29%) cited other barriers, and 14 firms made no response.

The survey questioned 'Would you be interested in free advice/ training using information technology to develop aspects of your business (please tick as appropriate)'. The 525 responses to this question determined the following positive interests:

- 94 firms (18%), business planning
- 105 firms (20%), marketing/sales
- 83 firms (16%), customer services
- 54 firms (10%), financial management
- 29 firms (6%), import/export
- 127 firms (24%), IT training
- 33 firms (6%), other

Nine firms made no response.

As the questionnaire format was developed, the list of business aspects grew to include many of those now listed within Appendix 4. The format also changed, to ask specifically about the training and support that would help the owner/manager to take forward business' objectives and then to ask specifically about aspects to help its employees. By asking about aspects twice in this way, UPBEAT noted that more assistance was requested by the owner/managers.

Appendix 3
Surveying firms, reviewing what could have helped

Gathering the views of microbusinesses is crucial to ensuring that locally available services are effective because they are based on current knowledge of what would assist in protecting business viability and local jobs.

Microbusinesses should be chosen randomly for surveys. This, along with objectivity when filling in the questionnaires, is key to a meaningful result. Objectivity requires strict levels of business confidentiality and high levels of impartiality. It is not acceptable to limit areas of potential interest to those for which the surveyor's organisation offers business support service. The questionnaire that follows therefore encourages thought on a broad range of business aspects. Firms' details should be held in confidence and no employer or organisation should be identified by name.

Those surveying microbusinesses need to make it clear why the survey is being undertaken. This becomes ever more important, as the number of surveys increases and microbusinesses have less time spare to respond. The survey process can assist those being questioned by encouraging them to look back over their last year. Their thoughts can be stimulated regarding ways in which they could perhaps have organised things better. It can help them to review their work, to see where business improvements were made by seeking assistance outside their firms, and to acknowledge to themselves, with hindsight, where such assistance would have helped if it had been available and had been taken up.

The survey questionnaire, as in this Appendix, has been designed for use during a structured interview, by the interviewer, with microbusinesses. However, if resources do not permit one-to-one discussions, the questions can equally satisfactorily be completed by post or telephone through the colleges. Further invaluable information could be gained by recording the interviews, although both parties must agree to this.

The questionnaire references three different sources of assistance to microbusinesses.

- external training bodies: for example, colleges and private commercial training organisations

- external advisers: for example, professional advisers (like accountants) who sell services on a commercial basis, college mentors and Business Link advisers

- external authorities: for example local enforcement agencies and state-funded, national helplines acting as information sources

Question 3 itemises the key administration tasks and problem areas addressed by most organisations. The tasks are the 'indirect' ones which are common to organisations across many sectors and can take a disproportionate amount of resource. Question 4 covers the 'direct' tasks, which are specific to the 'production and delivery' of each organisation's business, product and service. Organisations which effectively fulfil their 'indirect' tasks, generally have more resource left for their 'direct' productive tasks.

Where questions require responses in range 1 to 5, 1 is low and 5 is high. Some questions may not be relevant to a particular smaller firm in which case they should record n/a against the question.

Those being surveyed may identify further elements where training or other support could be beneficial, or perhaps suggest ways in which local provision to local workplaces could be improved. If the firms are surveyed initially and again say six months later, positive changes in survey responses could indicate, for instance, easier trading conditions or improved training and support services, due to effective action on prompt analysis of the initial survey's findings.

A survey questionnaire

Example questions 1 and 2. Staffing levels

Q1 How many staff work in your organisation currently?
Full time   Part time

Q2 Does your organisation have the same staffing levels and hours as it did about this time last year, including seasonal staff
(tick Yes or No, as appropriate)   Yes   No

If your answer to Q2 is 'Yes', have the hours worked been reduced?
(tick Yes or No, as appropriate)   Yes   No

If your answer to Q2 is 'No', please give the changes in staffing levels
No. of full-time jobs less   No. of full-time jobs more
No. of part-time jobs less   No. of part-time jobs more

Example question 3. Indirect tasks

Question 3 itemises those key 'administration' tasks and key problem areas which are addressed by most organisations. The tasks are the 'indirect' ones which can take a disproportionate amount of smaller organisations' resource. Organisations which effectively fulfil their 'indirect' tasks, generally have more resource left for their 'direct' productive tasks which produce goods or provide services. The 'direct' tasks are specific to an organisation's business, but very often the indirect tasks are common to organisations across many sectors.

For questions in this section (3.1 to 3.16), five additional questions are asked, to determine how the firm overcame a problem related to the topic of the main question, or would do so, in hindsight. The five additional questions are as follows.

- Did training by an external body help to ease this task?
  Yes/No   If Yes, how much training? (enter 1 to 5)

- Did an external adviser help to ease this task?
  Yes/No   If Yes, how much training? (enter 1 to 5)

- Did an external authority provide information which eased this task?
  Yes/No   If Yes, how much training? (enter 1 to 5)

- With hindsight, would some or more training have eased this task?
  Yes/No   If Yes, how much training? (enter 1 to 5)

- With hindsight, would this task have been eased by some or more advice or information?
  Yes/No   If Yes, how much training? (enter 1 to 5)

3.1 Have you spent increasing resource in marketing the organisation and what it offers, and in monitoring competitors?
  Yes/No   If Yes, how much of a problem has this been? (enter 1 to 5)

3.2 Have you needed to change the status of your organisation (for instance from charitable status to incorporated status)?
  Yes/No   If Yes, how much of a problem has this been? (enter 1 to 5)

3.3 Have you had difficulty in securing new contracts to supply other organisations ?
  Yes/No   If Yes, how much of a problem has this been? (enter 1 to 5)

3.4 Have you lost time in leasing premises or in achieving appropriate planning permission?
  Yes/No   If Yes, how much of a problem has this been? (enter 1 to 5)

3.5 Has time been lost unnecessarily in applying new employment regulations?
  Yes/No   If Yes, how much of a problem has this been? (enter 1 to 5)

3.6 Has time been lost unnecessarily in applying health and safety requirements?
  Yes/No   If Yes, how much of a problem has this been? (enter 1 to 5)

3.7 Has time been lost in gathering and collating details for tax return and trading account purposes?
  Yes/No   If Yes, how much of a problem has this been? (enter 1 to 5)

3.8 Due to reducing trade, have your standard sales terms needed to be revised or service levels reduced?
  Yes/No   If Yes, how much of a problem has this been? (enter 1 to 5)

3.9 Has time been lost on financial issues, debt chasing or revising expenditure plans?
  Yes/No   If Yes, how much of a problem has this been? (enter 1 to 5)

3.10 Has resource been wasted in getting relevant export documentation?
Yes/No   If Yes, how much of a problem has this been? (enter 1 to 5)

3.11 Has time been lost in understanding management standards,
like ISO 9000 or the Investor in People award?
Yes/No   If Yes, how much of a problem has this been? (enter 1 to 5)

3.12 Has time been lost unnecessarily during audits or assessments ?
Yes/No   If Yes, how much of a problem has this been? (enter 1 to 5)

3.13 Has time been wasted during the selection or
installation of computer facilities?
Yes/No   If Yes, how much of a problem has this been? (enter 1 to 5)

3.14 Are staff consistently needing to work on outside normal hours?
Yes/No   If Yes, how much of a problem has this been? (enter 1 to 5)

3.15 Has time been lost due to unanticipated staff turnover
and/or recruitment difficulties?
Yes/No   If Yes, how much of a problem has this been? (enter 1 to 5)

3.16 Has time been lost trying to find information and
assistance which is specific to your type of work?
Yes/No   If Yes, how much of a problem has this been? (enter 1 to 5)

Example question 4. Direct tasks

Question 4 covers the direct tasks, which will be specific to the
production and delivery of each different type of business.
The following question itemises those tasks which are directly
concerned with the production and delivery of your organisation's
products and services.

4.1 If the performing of indirect tasks had been made less time consuming
(see Questions 3.1–3.16 above), would the time saved be put to good
use on direct tasks?
Yes/No   If Yes, to what extent? (enter 1 to 5)   Any comments?

4.2 Did your organisation have training on the tasks directly concerned
with the production of its products and services in the last year?
Yes/No   If Yes, to what extent? (enter 1 to 5)   Any comments?

4.3 Did your organisation have assistance via a Business Link or Enterprise
Agency on the production or delivery of its products and services in
the last year?
Yes/No   If Yes, to what extent? (enter 1 to 5)   Any comments?

4.4 Did your organisation seek advice or information from a source other
than a Business Link or Enterprise Agency (e. g. from a specialist,

non-state funded, commercial supplier) on the tasks directly concerned with the production or delivery of its products and services in the last year?

Yes/No   If Yes, to what extent? (enter 1 to 5)   Any comments?

4.5 Did your organisation get assistance in improving real and sustainable profit and productivity levels in the last year?

Yes/No   If Yes, to what extent? (enter 1 to 5)   Any comments?

4.6 With hindsight over the last year, would additional training on direct tasks have been helpful to protecting jobs or growing the organisation?

Yes/No   If Yes, to what extent? (enter 1 to 5)   Any comments?

4.7 With hindsight, would your organisation have benefited from seeking additional advice or information in relation to the tasks directly concerned with the production of its products and services in the last year?

Yes/No   If Yes, to what extent? (enter 1 to 5)   Any comments?

Example questions 5–15. General questions

The following questions are to be completed as appropriate.

5 What is the status of your organisation (for instance, a limited company, charity, a community organisation limited by guarantee or a co-operative)?

6 Can your organisation call upon the resources of a larger one (perhaps a key client)?

7 What products and services does your particular organisation offer, and which sector does it trade in?

8 How many years has your organisation been established?

9 Do you sell usually to: a) other organisations or b) to the public, direct?

10 Is your organisation already in contact with a FE college? If so, describe shared activities (eg. use of computer facilities, staff on day or block release, ad-hoc training and so on).

11 Do you have reservations to being in contact with your local FE college? If so, why?

12 Do you have reservations to being in contact with your local Business Link or Enterprise Agency? If so, why?

13 Any additional comment?

14 If you wish, please give the name of your organisation, and a contact name and telephone number.

15 Date questionnaire completed.

Thank you for your co-operation.

Appendix 4

Linking lifelong learning to better regulation

Relating regulatory requirements to learning needs

Commercial and employment-related regulations have accumulated and become more complicated over the years; they now form an essential aspect of learning within the workplace. The creation of the European Union's Single Market has added much to the complication in the efforts to 'harmonise' legal systems across Member States.

States do recognise that smaller employers' costs are increased in trying to understand and implement new regulatory requirements. The UK's Regulatory Impact Unit[23] lies within the Cabinet Office, which gives an indication of its importance. A Better Regulation Task Force has been formed, independent of government and supported by the Cabinet Office, to assist in the reform of current regulation and the scrutiny of proposed regulation. Its recent work,[24] notes that small firms suffer a disproportionate burden in complying with regulation, so are often at a competitive disadvantage with larger firms. This confirms earlier work undertaken by the European Commission in relation to all Member States.[25]

Official initiatives

Many official initiatives have been launched in the European Union and in Member States over the years, with the stated objective of improving the regulatory systems. Few have helped smaller trading firms, perhaps because of a lack of political will or parliamentary time. One approach to reducing the burden on microbusinesses has been the introduction of small business exemptions, where a particular set of regulations does not apply to independent organisations with under a given number of employees. Such exemptions apply, for instance, to trade union recognition provisions. Although they may be the only solution to the current complexity of regulation, they are discriminatory and may form a barrier to growth. Practical assistance is needed in this area.

Promoting co-ordination

'Better regulation' initiatives over the years have focused more on 'deregulation' in trading licences to create 'free markets', than on encouraging co-ordination between state departments.

Proper co-ordination between State departments could benefit rational competition; for instance by encouraging DfEE and DTI to make common, clear announcements to employers regarding new regulations and ensure that practical assistance to firms is arranged for each UK region and locality.

Effective co-ordination between government departments could also help to improve the current audit and assessment situation. Sets of regulations with individual audit and inspection regimes continue to emanate from many parts of the State, sometimes stimulated by their counterparts in the European Commission. In the UK, the DTI's Corporate Affairs Division maintains the financial audit, which is a statutory requirement for incorporated companies, but other departments and divisions control mandatory requirements relating, for instance, to health and safety, food hygiene, planning, environmental issues, VAT and other taxes, and employment laws, including working-time regulations and the national minimum wage.

Voluntary standards

Another key issue is the credibility of voluntary management standards and their assessment infrastructures in 'free markets' involving a mix of government departments and private concerns. For example, the DTI Standards Division has an official interest in maintaining voluntary, international standards for quality, although the officially instigated Investor in People Award, the voluntary national training standard, is privatised. The sustained credibility of these and other voluntary systems can be key to firms, as their certification may be a requirement to secure work with larger organisations or the State.

If regulations are well drafted, well thought through and well presented, an organisation's profit or resource is tapped to better effect. Where there is poor regulation, like the EU's public procurement regime, it fails to ensure that small orders can be secured by microbusinesses – to the detriment of many areas of high unemployment throughout the European Union.

References

1 *The Small Business Service: a public consultation*. URN 99/815 DTI, June 1999. Proposals for the creation of the Small Business Service are subject to consultation, and to Parliamentary approval of the Government's finalised proposals. Further information can be found via www.businessadviceonline.org.uk

2 The Ufi Ltd website (www.UfILtd.co.uk) is the main information point for Ufi and contains official releases and documents. Ecotec's UfI website (www.ecotec.com/UfI) provides newsletters, detailed information on UfI-related development/pilot projects and summaries of UfI-type activity by region.

3 White Paper *Learning to Succeed*. DfEE, 1999 (www.dfee.gov.uk/post16). Annex 1 of the White Paper provides a 'Transition plan for post-16 education and training and local delivery of support to microbusinesses'.

4 Teaching and Higher Education Act 1998, Part III (*Right to time off for study or training*), effective from 1 September 1999.

5 DfEE *Employment news*, March/April 1999.

6 *Competitiveness through partnerships with people*. URN 97/838, DTI and DfEE, 1997; Working for the future. URN 99/514, DTI, 1999.

7 *How colleges work with small businesses: a survey report* (Learning and Skills Development Agency, 2000), the ADAPT/FESME VCU survey report

8 The Learning and Skills Development Agency (formerly FEDA) is a strategic national resource for the development of policy and practice in post-16 education and training. The Agency publishes a wide range of publications relating to post-16 policy, research and quality improvement and inclusive partnership work. Further information can be obtained by e-mailing enquiries@LSagency.org.uk or by writing to Learning and Skills Development Agency publications, 3 Citadel Place, Tinworth Street, London SE11 5EF.

9 *Finance for microbusinesses: a fifth report*. Bank of England, 1998.

10 *CAB evidence: job insecurity*. ISBN 0 906072 15 8, National Association of Citizens Advice Bureaux, 1993. Another useful, independent source is ACAS.

11 The quarterly reports by the Small Business Research Trust have formed a useful source of microbusinesses' views over the years. The Nat.West/SBRT *Quarterly survey of small business in Britain* (1996; vol. 12, No. 1 and 1998; Vol. 14, No. 1), for instance, looked into the disproportionate effects of compliance costs on microbusinesses. For further information, contact SBRT, School of Management, The Open University, Walton Hall, Milton Keynes MK7 6AA (tel: 01908 655831).

12 *Barriers to growth*. A report by the Enterprise Group of the Institute of Chartered Accountants in England and Wales, 1996.

13 The Marchmont Project (www.lifelonglearning.ac.uk) is a source of project-related information.

14 *ADAPT: Use of S/NVQ Training for SMEs*. DfEE, 1999.

15 Hughes, M and Gray S Promoting learning in SMEs (FEDA, 1998)

16 The project entitled CESaME (Centre for Enabling Small and Medium Enterprises) received European funds within the Leonardo da Vinci programme to lay the basis for a pan-European network of Business Coaches to support microbusinesses and generate a database of information and training materials, for smaller firms and for Business Coaches. The Leonardo da Vinci programme was curtailed but CESaME's ideas are being taken forward by Materials Director Mike Bolton through informing the ADAPT project and developing a diagnostic package. Mike Bolton may be contacted at mike.bolton@virgin.net.

17 The Institute of Business Advisers (www.iba.org.uk) was incorporated in 1989 to provide professional development for people working in a business support role, for instance through the Enterprise Agencies, TECs and Business Links. The IBA defines four roles within its professional structure:

- business advisers who provide 'independent, impartial and confidential information and guidance to potential and established businesses, based upon substantial business experience and current knowledge of related factors, so that clients may learn and benefit from their advice in their subsequent actions'

- business counsellors who undertake 'a process by which business problems are diagnosed and resolved in such a way that the client learns not only how to overcome their current difficulties, or exploit their opportunities, but also how to tackle similar situations in the future'

- business mentors who stimulate 'an on-going, long-term business counselling relationship between an experienced business adviser and a client which covers a diverse range of topics as a business develops'

- training for owners, managers and directors of small firms is 'a group activity focusing on specific aspects of the management spectrum led by a qualified and experienced business adviser'.

18 Teaching and Higher Education Act. 1998, Part III (Right to time off for study or training), effective from 1 September 1999. This an example of a piece of legislation that guides employers towards the NTO central council, to be redirected to 'the NTO for a specific sector'. It provides a list of over 90 specified qualification awarding bodies for the regulations; these are daunting research and evaluation tasks for most employers. Funding and good practice details are also provided but the funding relates to training for the young person and no guidance is given to assist the smaller employer in covering the cost of management time away from productive work to evaluate training options with the young person or to organise work so that the young person can be released effectively. Unless guidance is provided on how productivity can be increased to cover such costs, the employer's business and job provision are degraded. (www. dfee.gov.uk/tfst.htm; 1999).

19 This may determine subject areas that apply to all types of micro-businesses to some degree, for instance IT-related training, management technique training, finance and accounting, and clerical, administration and telesales. Training may lead to qualifications within an OCN scheme or the NVQ scheme.

20 This example is chosen because one of Ufi Ltd's aims is to work with business and trade unions to support and develop skills in the workplace, including improved provision for small firms (University for Industry *Pathfinder prospectus*. Ref. PP80D10/33394/398/353, DfEE, 1998). On first sight, the Employment NTO's training and development standards may not directly assist employers in microbusinesses to understand job evaluation techniques; how to determine fair and sound performance measurements; or how to adapt to collective relationships with staff represented by unions. Microbusiness employers, especially those wishing to grow to the size at which union representation rights apply (Employment Relations Act, 1999), may well need assistance in understanding how best to adapt their work practices to gain mutual benefit through worker representation and collaborative processes. The Employment NTO can be contacted by e-mail on info@empnto.co.uk

21 Clustering can now follow a strict methodology and incorporate recent philosophies (*The clusters approach*, SE/1542/Mar 98, Scottish Enterprise, 1998), but is used here in the form of groupings which share common interests. For instance, a cluster of microbusinesses can have the common bond of having purchased from the same computer software or courseware supplier or training establishment, or could serve the same customer or types of customer. Clustering can also enable those within it to collate and share market and economic information to mutual benefit. This may also enable the cluster to share such information with those with regional influence and at national and government levels, perhaps in conjunction with the Small Business Service.

22 The details on Tables 1 and 2 relate to the private sector, and are extracted from the statistical bulletin, *Small and Medium Enterprise (SME) statistics for the United Kingdom 1998*. SME Statistics Unit, DTI URN 99/92, 1999. This publication should be referenced for further details of these figures and in relation to discrepancies in the totals. All details are from the DTI's publication's Table 3 for Start-98 (January 1998), except the turnover/enterprise details, which are from Table 4, and the two sets of annual percentage figures, which are from Table 25.

23 Information regarding the Regulatory Impact Unit's work can currently be found on website www.cabinet-office.gov.uk. The RIU was formerly the Better Regulation Unit and, before that, the Deregulation Unit.

24 *Regulation and small firms progress report*. Better Regulation Task Force: Cabinet Office, July 1999.

25 *National regulations affecting products in the internal market: a cause for concern*. III/2185–EN/final, European Commission, 1996.

Contact addresses

The Employment NTO can be contacted by e-mail on info@empnto.co.uk

FEDA is now the Learning and Skills Development Agency.
Its website address is www.LSagency.org.uk

RJ Pengelly can be contacted by e-mail on nweu@calemcal.demon.co.uk

Other websites

The Institute of Business Advisers www.iba.org.uk

The National Association of Citizens Advice Bureaux www.nacab.org.uk

The NTO National Council www.nto-nc.org

The English Regional Development Agencies website addresses are:

- Advantage West Midlands www.advantage-westmidlands.co.uk
- East Midlands Development Agency www.emda.org.uk
- East of England Development Agency www.eeda.org.uk
- North West Development Agency www.nwda.co.uk
- One North East www.onenortheast.co.uk
- South East England Development Agency www.seeda.co.uk
- South West England Development Agency
  www.southwestengland.co.uk
- Yorkshire Forward www.yorkshire-forward.com

The work of the Regulatory Impact Unit can currently be found
on the Cabinet Office website on www.cabinet-office.gov.uk.

For further information on the Small Business Research Trust,
contact SBRT, School of Management, The Open University,
Walton Hall, Milton Keynes MK7 6AA (tel: 01908 655831)

The Small Business Service is an agency of the
Department of Trade and Industry. Its website
can be accessed through DTI's on www.dti.gov.uk

The Ufi Ltd www.ufiltd.co.uk.

Ecotec's Ufi website www.ecotec.com/Ufi

The Welsh Development Agency www.wda.co.uk